Birds of Passage by Henry Wadsworth Longfellow

BIRDS OF PASSAGE

FLIGHT THE FIRST

. . come i gru van cantando lor lai,
Facendo in aer di se lunga riga. -- DANTE

BIRDS OF PASSAGE

Black shadows fall
From the lindens tall,
That lift aloft their massive wall

Against the southern sky;

And from the realms
Of the shadowy elms
A tide-like darkness overwhelms
The fields that round us lie.

But the night is fair,
And everywhere
A warm, soft vapor fills the air,
And distant sounds seem near,

And above, in the light
Of the star-lit night,
Swift birds of passage wing their flight
Through the dewy atmosphere.

I hear the beat
Of their pinions fleet,
As from the land of snow and sleet
They seek a southern lea.

I hear the cry
Of their voices high
Falling dreamily through the sky,
But their forms I cannot see.

O, say not so!
Those sounds that flow
In murmurs of delight and woe
Come not from wings of birds.

They are the throngs
Of the poet's songs,
Murmurs of pleasures, and pains, and wrongs,
The sound of winged words.

This is the cry
Of souls, that high
On toiling, beating pinions, fly,
Seeking a warmer clime,

From their distant flight
Through realms of light
It falls into our world of night,
With the murmuring sound of rhyme.

PROMETHEUS

OR THE POET'S FORETHOUGHT

Of Prometheus, how undaunted
On Olympus' shining bastions
His audacious foot he planted,
Myths are told and songs are chanted,
Full of promptings and suggestions.

Beautiful is the tradition
Of that flight through heavenly portals,
The old classic superstition
Of the theft and the transmission
Of the fire of the Immortals!

First the deed of noble daring,
Born of heavenward aspiration,
Then the fire with mortals sharing,
Then the vulture,--the despairing
Cry of pain on crags Caucasian.

All is but a symbol painted
Of the Poet, Prophet, Seer;
Only those are crowned and sainted
Who with grief have been acquainted,
Making nations nobler, freer.

In their feverish exultations,
In their triumph and their yearning,
In their passionate pulsations,
In their words among the nations,
The Promethean fire is burning.

Shall it, then, be unavailing,
All this toil for human culture?
Through the cloud-rack, dark and trailing,
Must they see above them sailing
O'er life's barren crags the vulture?

Such a fate as this was Dante's,
By defeat and exile maddened;
Thus were Milton and Cervantes,
Nature's priests and Corybantes,
By affliction touched and saddened.

But the glories so transcendent

That around their memories cluster,
And, on all their steps attendant,
Make their darkened lives resplendent
With such gleams of inward lustre!

All the melodies mysterious,
Through the dreary darkness chanted;
Thoughts in attitudes imperious,
Voices soft, and deep, and serious,
Words that whispered, songs that haunted!

All the soul in rapt suspension,
All the quivering, palpitating
Chords of life in utmost tension,
With the fervor of invention,
With the rapture of creating!

Ah, Prometheus! heaven-scaling!
In such hours of exultation
Even the faintest heart, unquailing,
Might behold the vulture sailing
Round the cloudy crags Caucasian!

Though to all there is not given
Strength for such sublime endeavor,
Thus to scale the walls of heaven,
And to leaven with fiery leaven
All the hearts of men for ever;

Yet all bards, whose hearts unblighted
Honor and believe the presage,
Hold aloft their torches lighted,
Gleaming through the realms benighted,
As they onward bear the message!

EPIMETHEUS

OR THE POET'S AFTERTHOUGHT

Have I dreamed? or was it real,
What I saw as in a vision,
When to marches hymeneal
In the land of the Ideal
Moved my thought o'er Fields Elysian?

What! are these the guests whose glances

Seemed like sunshine gleaming round me?
These the wild, bewildering fancies,
That with dithyrambic dances
As with magic circles bound me?

Ah! how cold are their caresses!
Pallid cheeks, and haggard bosoms!
Spectral gleam their snow-white dresses,
And from loose dishevelled tresses
Fall the hyacinthine blossoms!

O my songs! whose winsome measures
Filled my heart with secret rapture!
Children of my golden leisures!
Must even your delights and pleasures
Fade and perish with the capture?

Fair they seemed, those songs sonorous,
When they came to me unbidden;
Voices single, and in chorus,
Like the wild birds singing o'er us
In the dark of branches hidden.

Disenchantment! Disillusion!
Must each noble aspiration
Come at last to this conclusion,
Jarring discord, wild confusion,
Lassitude, renunciation?

Not with steeper fall nor faster,
From the sun's serene dominions,
Not through brighter realms nor vaster,
In swift ruin and disaster,
Icarus fell with shattered pinions!

Sweet Pandora! dear Pandora!
Why did mighty Jove create thee
Coy as Thetis, fair as Flora,
Beautiful as young Aurora,
If to win thee is to hate thee?

No, not hate thee! for this feeling
Of unrest and long resistance
Is but passionate appealing,
A prophetic whisper stealing
O'er the chords of our existence.

Him whom thou dost once enamour,

Thou, beloved, never leavest;
In life's discord, strife, and clamor,
Still he feels thy spell of glamour;
Him of Hope thou ne'er bereavest.

Weary hearts by thee are lifted,
Struggling souls by thee are strengthened,
Clouds of fear asunder rifted,
Truth from falsehood cleansed and sifted,
Lives, like days in summer, lengthened!

Therefore art thou ever clearer,
O my Sibyl, my deceiver!
For thou makest each mystery clearer,
And the unattained seems nearer,
When thou fillest my heart with fever!

Muse of all the Gifts and Graces!
Though the fields around us wither,
There are ampler realms and spaces,
Where no foot has left its traces:
Let us turn and wander thither!

THE LADDER OF ST. AUGUSTINE

Saint Augustine! well hast thou said,
That of our vices we can frame
A ladder, if we will but tread
Beneath our feet each deed of shame!

All common things, each day's events,
That with the hour begin and end,
Our pleasures and our discontents,
Are rounds by which we may ascend.

The low desire, the base design,
That makes another's virtues less;
The revel of the ruddy wine,
And all occasions of excess;

The longing for ignoble things;
The strife for triumph more than truth;
The hardening of the heart, that brings
Irreverence for the dreams of youth;

All thoughts of ill; all evil deeds,

That have their root in thoughts of ill;
Whatever hinders or impedes
The action of the nobler will;--

All these must first be trampled down
Beneath our feet, if we would gain
In the bright fields of fair renown
The right of eminent domain.

We have not wings, we cannot soar;
But we have feet to scale and climb
By slow degrees, by more and more,
The cloudy summits of our time.

The mighty pyramids of stone
That wedge-like cleave the desert airs,
When nearer seen, and better known,
Are but gigantic flights of stairs.

The distant mountains, that uprear
Their solid bastions to the skies,
Are crossed by pathways, that appear
As we to higher levels rise.

The heights by great men reached and kept
Were not attained by sudden flight,
But they, while their companions slept,
Were toiling upward in the night.

Standing on what too long we bore
With shoulders bent and downcast eyes,
We may discern--unseen before--
A path to higher destinies.

Nor deem the irrevocable Past,
As wholly wasted, wholly vain,
If, rising on its wrecks, at last
To something nobler we attain.

THE PHANTOM SHIP

In Mather's Magnalia Christi,
Of the old colonial time,
May be found in prose the legend
That is here set down in rhyme.

A ship sailed from New Haven,
And the keen and frosty airs,
That filled her sails at parting,
Were heavy with good men's prayers.

"O Lord! if it be thy pleasure"--
Thus prayed the old divine--
"To bury our friends in the ocean,
Take them, for they are thine!"

But Master Lamberton muttered,
And under his breath said he,
"This ship is so crank and walty
I fear our grave she will be!"

And the ships that came from England,
When the winter months were gone,
Brought no tidings of this vessel
Nor of Master Lamberton.

This put the people to praying
That the Lord would let them hear
What in his greater wisdom
He had done with friends so dear.

And at last their prayers were answered:--
It was in the month of June,
An hour before the sunset
Of a windy afternoon,

When, steadily steering landward,
A ship was seen below,
And they knew it was Lamberton, Master,
Who sailed so long ago.

On she came, with a cloud of canvas,
Right against the wind that blew,
Until the eye could distinguish
The faces of the crew.

Then fell her straining topmasts,
Hanging tangled in the shrouds,
And her sails were loosened and lifted,
And blown away like clouds.

And the masts, with all their rigging,
Fell slowly, one by one,
And the hulk dilated and vanished,

As a sea-mist in the sun!

And the people who saw this marvel
Each said unto his friend,
That this was the mould of their vessel,
And thus her tragic end.

And the pastor of the village
Gave thanks to God in prayer,
That, to quiet their troubled spirits,
He had sent this Ship of Air.

THE WARDEN OF THE CINQUE PORTS

A mist was driving down the British Channel,
The day was just begun,
And through the window-panes, on floor and panel,
Streamed the red autumn sun.

It glanced on flowing flag and rippling pennon,
And the white sails of ships;
And, from the frowning rampart, the black cannon
Hailed it with feverish lips.

Sandwich and Romney, Hastings, Hithe, and Dover
Were all alert that day,
To see the French war-steamers speeding over,
When the fog cleared away.

Sullen and silent, and like couchant lions,
Their cannon, through the night,
Holding their breath, had watched, in grim defiance,
The sea-coast opposite.

And now they roared at drum-beat from their stations
On every citadel;
Each answering each, with morning salutations,
That all was well.

And down the coast, all taking up the burden,
Replied the distant forts,
As if to summon from his sleep the Warden
And Lord of the Cinque Ports.

Him shall no sunshine from the fields of azure,
No drum-beat from the wall,

No morning gun from the black fort's embrasure,
Awaken with its call!

No more, surveying with an eye impartial
The long line of the coast,
Shall the gaunt figure of the old Field Marshal
Be seen upon his post!

For in the night, unseen, a single warrior,
In sombre harness mailed,
Dreaded of man, and surnamed the Destroyer,
The rampart wall has scaled.

He passed into the chamber of the sleeper,
The dark and silent room,
And as he entered, darker grew, and deeper,
The silence and the gloom.

He did not pause to parley or dissemble,
But smote the Warden hoar;
Ah! what a blow! that made all England tremble
And groan from shore to shore.

Meanwhile, without, the surly cannon waited,
The sun rose bright o'erhead;
Nothing in Nature's aspect intimated
That a great man was dead.

HAUNTED HOUSES

All houses wherein men have lived and died
Are haunted houses. Through the open doors
The harmless phantoms on their errands glide,
With feet that make no sound upon the floors.

We meet them at the door-way, on the stair,
Along the passages they come and go,
Impalpable impressions on the air,
A sense of something moving to and fro.

There are more guests at table, than the hosts
Invited; the illuminated hall
Is thronged with quiet, inoffensive ghosts,
As silent as the pictures on the wall.

The stranger at my fireside cannot see

The forms I see, nor hear the sounds I hear;
He but perceives what is; while unto me
All that has been is visible and clear.

We have no title-deeds to house or lands;
Owners and occupants of earlier dates
From graves forgotten stretch their dusty hands,
And hold in mortmain still their old estates.

The spirit-world around this world of sense
Floats like an atmosphere, and everywhere
Wafts through these earthly mists and vapors dense
A vital breath of more ethereal air.

Our little lives are kept in equipoise
By opposite attractions and desires;
The struggle of the instinct that enjoys,
And the more noble instinct that aspires.

These perturbations, this perpetual jar
Of earthly wants and aspirations high,
Come from the influence of an unseen star,
An undiscovered planet in our sky.

And as the moon from some dark gate of cloud
Throws o'er the sea a floating bridge of light,
Across whose trembling planks our fancies crowd
Into the realm of mystery and night,--

So from the world of spirits there descends
A bridge of light, connecting it with this,
O'er whose unsteady floor, that sways and bends,
Wander our thoughts above the dark abyss.

IN THE CHURCHYARD AT CAMBRIDGE

In the village churchyard she lies,
Dust is in her beautiful eyes,
No more she breathes, nor feels, nor stirs;
At her feet and at her head
Lies a slave to attend the dead,
But their dust is white as hers.

Was she a lady of high degree,
So much in love with the vanity
And foolish pomp of this world of ours?

Or was it Christian charity,
And lowliness and humility,
The richest and rarest of all dowers?

Who shall tell us? No one speaks;
No color shoots into those cheeks,
Either of anger or of pride,
At the rude question we have asked;
Nor will the mystery be unmasked
By those who are sleeping at her side.

Hereafter?--And do you think to look
On the terrible pages of that Book
To find her failings, faults, and errors?
Ah, you will then have other cares,
In your own short-comings and despairs,
In your own secret sins and terrors!

THE EMPEROR'S BIRD'S-NEST

Once the Emperor Charles of Spain,
With his swarthy, grave commanders,
I forget in what campaign,
Long besieged, in mud and rain,
Some old frontier town of Flanders.

Up and down the dreary camp,
In great boots of Spanish leather,
Striding with a measured tramp,
These Hidalgos, dull and damp,
Cursed the Frenchmen, cursed the weather.

Thus as to and fro they went,
Over upland and through hollow,
Giving their impatience vent,
Perched upon the Emperor's tent,
In her nest, they spied a swallow.

Yes, it was a swallow's nest,
Built of clay and hair of horses,
Mane, or tail, or dragoon's crest,
Found on hedge-rows east and west,
After skirmish of the forces.

Then an old Hidalgo said,
As he twirled his gray mustachio,

"Sure this swallow overhead
Thinks the Emperor's tent a shed,
And the Emperor but a Macho!"

Hearing his imperial name
Coupled with those words of malice,
Half in anger, half in shame,
Forth the great campaigner came
Slowly from his canvas palace.

"Let no hand the bird molest,"
Said he solemnly, "nor hurt her!"
Adding then, by way of jest,
"Golondrina is my guest,
'Tis the wife of some deserter!"

Swift as bowstring speeds a shaft,
Through the camp was spread the rumor,
And the soldiers, as they quaffed
Flemish beer at dinner, laughed
At the Emperor's pleasant humor.

So unharmed and unafraid
Sat the swallow still and brooded,
Till the constant cannonade
Through the walls a breach had made,
And the siege was thus concluded.

Then the army, elsewhere bent,
Struck its tents as if disbanding,
Only not the Emperor's tent,
For he ordered, ere he went,
Very curtly, "Leave it standing!"

So it stood there all alone,
Loosely flapping, torn and tattered,
Till the brood was fledged and flown,
Singing o'er those walls of stone
Which the cannon-shot had shattered.

THE TWO ANGELS

Two angels, one of Life and one of Death,
Passed o'er our village as the morning broke;
The dawn was on their faces, and beneath,
The sombre houses hearsed with plumes of smoke.

Their attitude and aspect were the same,
Alike their features and their robes of white;
But one was crowned with amaranth, as with flame,
And one with asphodels, like flakes of light.

I saw them pause on their celestial way;
Then said I, with deep fear and doubt oppressed,
"Beat not so loud, my heart, lest thou betray
The place where thy beloved are at rest!"

And he who wore the crown of asphodels,
Descending, at my door began to knock,
And my soul sank within me, as in wells
The waters sink before an earthquake's shock.

I recognized the nameless agony,
The terror and the tremor and the pain,
That oft before had filled or haunted me,
And now returned with threefold strength again.

The door I opened to my heavenly guest,
And listened, for I thought I heard God's voice;
And, knowing whatsoe'er he sent was best,
Dared neither to lament nor to rejoice.

Then with a smile, that filled the house with light,
"My errand is not Death, but Life," he said;
And ere I answered, passing out of sight,
On his celestial embassy he sped.

'T was at thy door, O friend! and not at mine,
The angel with the amaranthine wreath,
Pausing, descended, and with voice divine,
Whispered a word that had a sound like Death.

Then fell upon the house a sudden gloom,
A shadow on those features fair and thin;
And softly, from that hushed and darkened room,
Two angels issued, where but one went in.

All is of God! If he but wave his hand,
The mists collect, the rain falls thick and loud,
Till, with a smile of light on sea and land,
Lo! he looks back from the departing cloud.

Angels of Life and Death alike are his;
Without his leave they pass no threshold o'er;

Who, then, would wish or dare, believing this,
Against his messengers to shut the door?

DAYLIGHT AND MOONLIGHT

In broad daylight, and at noon,
Yesterday I saw the moon
Sailing high, but faint and white,
As a school-boy's paper kite.

In broad daylight, yesterday,
I read a Poet's mystic lay;
And it seemed to me at most
As a phantom, or a ghost.

But at length the feverish day
Like a passion died away,
And the night, serene and still,
Fell on village, vale, and hill.

Then the moon, in all her pride,
Like a spirit glorified,
Filled and overflowed the night
With revelations of her light.

And the Poet's song again
Passed like music through my brain;
Night interpreted to me
All its grace and mystery.

THE JEWISH CEMETERY AT NEWPORT

How strange it seems! These Hebrews in their graves,
Close by the street of this fair seaport town,
Silent beside the never-silent waves,
At rest in all this moving up and down!

The trees are white with dust, that o'er their sleep
Wave their broad curtains in the south-wind's breath,
While underneath such leafy tents they keep
The long, mysterious Exodus of Death.

And these sepulchral stones, so old and brown,
That pave with level flags their burial-place,

Seem like the tablets of the Law, thrown down
And broken by Moses at the mountain's base.

The very names recorded here are strange,
Of foreign accent, and of different climes;
Alvares and Rivera interchange
With Abraham and Jacob of old times.

"Blessed be God! for he created Death!"
The mourners said, "and Death is rest and peace";
Then added, in the certainty of faith,
"And giveth Life that never more shall cease."

Closed are the portals of their Synagogue,
No Psalms of David now the silence break,
No Rabbi reads the ancient Decalogue
In the grand dialect the Prophets spake.

Gone are the living, but the dead remain,
And not neglected; for a hand unseen,
Scattering its bounty, like a summer rain,
Still keeps their graves and their remembrance green.

How came they here? What burst of Christian hate,
What persecution, merciless and blind,
Drove o'er the sea--that desert desolate--
These Ishmaels and Hagars of mankind?

They lived in narrow streets and lanes obscure,
Ghetto and Judenstrass, in mirk and mire;
Taught in the school of patience to endure
The life of anguish and the death of fire.

All their lives long, with the unleavened bread
And bitter herbs of exile and its fears,
The wasting famine of the heart they fed,
And slaked its thirst with marah of their tears.

Anathema maranatha! was the cry
That rang from town to town, from street to street;
At every gate the accursed Mordecai
Was mocked and jeered, and spurned by Christian feet.

Pride and humiliation hand in hand
Walked with them through the world where'er they went;
Trampled and beaten were they as the sand,
And yet unshaken as the continent.

For in the background figures vague and vast
Of patriarchs and of prophets rose sublime,
And all the great traditions of the Past
They saw reflected in the coming time.

And thus for ever with reverted look
The mystic volume of the world they read,
Spelling it backward, like a Hebrew book,
Till life became a Legend of the Dead.

But ah! what once has been shall be no more!
The groaning earth in travail and in pain
Brings forth its races, but does not restore,
And the dead nations never rise again.

OLIVER BASSELIN

In the Valley of the Vire
Still is seen an ancient mill,
With its gables quaint and queer,
And beneath the window-sill,
On the stone,
These words alone:
"Oliver Basselin lived here."

Far above it, on the steep,
Ruined stands the old Chateau;
Nothing but the donjon-keep
Left for shelter or for show.
Its vacant eyes
Stare at the skies,
Stare at the valley green and deep.

Once a convent, old and brown,
Looked, but ah! it looks no more,
From the neighboring hillside down
On the rushing and the roar
Of the stream
Whose sunny gleam
Cheers the little Norman town.

In that darksome mill of stone,
To the water's dash and din,
Careless, humble, and unknown,
Sang the poet Basselin
Songs that fill

That ancient mill
With a splendor of its own.

Never feeling of unrest
Broke the pleasant dream he dreamed;
Only made to be his nest,
All the lovely valley seemed;
No desire
Of soaring higher
Stirred or fluttered in his breast.

True, his songs were not divine;
Were not songs of that high art,
Which, as winds do in the pine,
Find an answer in each heart;
But the mirth
Of this green earth
Laughed and revelled in his line.

From the alehouse and the inn,
Opening on the narrow street,
Came the loud, convivial din,
Singing and applause of feet,
The laughing lays
That in those days
Sang the poet Basselin.

In the castle, cased in steel,
Knights, who fought at Agincourt,
Watched and waited, spur on heel;
But the poet sang for sport
Songs that rang
Another clang,
Songs that lowlier hearts could feel.

In the convent, clad in gray,
Sat the monks in lonely cells,
Paced the cloisters, knelt to pray,
And the poet heard their bells;
But his rhymes
Found other chimes,
Nearer to the earth than they.

Gone are all the barons bold,
Gone are all the knights and squires,
Gone the abbot stern and cold,
And the brotherhood of friars;
Not a name

Remains to fame,
From those mouldering days of old!

But the poet's memory here
Of the landscape makes a part;
Like the river, swift and clear,
Flows his song through many a heart;
Haunting still
That ancient mill,
In the Valley of the Vire.

VICTOR GALBRAITH

Under the walls of Monterey
At daybreak the bugles began to play,
Victor Galbraith!
In the mist of the morning damp and gray,
These were the words they seemed to say:
"Come forth to thy death,
Victor Galbraith!"

Forth he came, with a martial tread;
Firm was his step, erect his head;
Victor Galbraith,
He who so well the bugle played,
Could not mistake the words it said:
"Come forth to thy death,
Victor Galbraith!"

He looked at the earth, he looked at the sky,
He looked at the files of musketry,
Victor Galbraith!
And he said, with a steady voice and eye,
"Take good aim; I am ready to die!"
Thus challenges death
Victor Galbraith.

Twelve fiery tongues flashed straight and red,
Six leaden balls on their errand sped;
Victor Galbraith
Falls to the ground, but he is not dead;
His name was not stamped on those balls of lead,
And they only scath
Victor Galbraith.

Three balls are in his breast and brain,

But he rises out of the dust again,
Victor Galbraith!
The water he drinks has a bloody stain;
"O kill me, and put me out of my pain!"
In his agony prayeth
Victor Galbraith.

Forth dart once more those tongues of flame,
And the bugler has died a death of shame,
Victor Galbraith!
His soul has gone back to whence it came,
And no one answers to the name,
When the Sergeant saith,
"Victor Galbraith!"

Under the walls of Monterey
By night a bugle is heard to play,
Victor Galbraith!
Through the mist of the valley damp and gray
The sentinels hear the sound, and say,
"That is the wraith
Of Victor Galbraith!"

MY LOST YOUTH

Often I think of the beautiful town
That is seated by the sea;
Often in thought go up and down
The pleasant streets of that dear old town,
And my youth comes back to me.
And a verse of a Lapland song
Is haunting my memory still:
"A boy's will is the wind's will,
And the thoughts of youth are long, long thoughts."

I can see the shadowy lines of its trees,
And catch, in sudden gleams,
The sheen of the far-surrounding seas,
And islands that were the Hersperides
Of all my boyish dreams.
And the burden of that old song,
It murmurs and whispers still:
"A boy's will is the wind's will,
And the thoughts of youth are long, long thoughts."

I remember the black wharves and the slips,

And the sea-tides tossing free;
And Spanish sailors with bearded lips,
And the beauty and mystery of the ships,
And the magic of the sea.
And the voice of that wayward song
Is singing and saying still:
"A boy's will is the wind's will,
And the thoughts of youth are long, long thoughts."

I remember the bulwarks by the shore,
And the fort upon the hill;
The sunrise gun, with its hollow roar,
The drum-beat repeated o'er and o'er,
And the bugle wild and shrill.
And the music of that old song
Throbs in my memory still:
"A boy's will is the wind's will,
And the thoughts of youth are long, long thoughts."

I remember the sea-fight far away,
How it thundered o'er the tide!
And the dead captains, as they lay
In their graves, o'erlooking the tranquil bay,
Where they in battle died.
And the sound of that mournful song
Goes through me with a thrill:
"A boy's will is the wind's will,
And the thoughts of youth are long, long thoughts."

I can see the breezy dome of groves,
The shadows of Deering's Woods;
And the friendships old and the early loves
Come back with a sabbath sound, as of doves
In quiet neighborhoods.
And the verse of that sweet old song,
It flutters and murmurs still:
"A boy's will is the wind's will,
And the thoughts of youth are long, long thoughts."

I remember the gleams and glooms that dart
Across the schoolboy's brain;
The song and the silence in the heart,
That in part are prophecies, and in part
Are longings wild and vain.
And the voice of that fitful song
Sings on, and is never still:
"A boy's will is the wind's will,
And the thoughts of youth are long, long thoughts."

There are things of which I may not speak;
There are dreams that cannot die;
There are thoughts that make the strong heart weak,
And bring a pallor into the cheek,
And a mist before the eye.
And the words of that fatal song
Come over me like a chill:
"A boy's will is the wind's will,
And the thoughts of youth are long, long thoughts."

Strange to me now are the forms I meet
When I visit the dear old town;
But the native air is pure and sweet,
And the trees that o'ershadow each well-known street,
As they balance up and down,
Are singing the beautiful song,
Are sighing and whispering still:
"A boy's will is the wind's will,
And the thoughts of youth are long, long thoughts."

And Deering's Woods are fresh and fair,
And with joy that is almost pain
My heart goes back to wander there,
And among the dreams of the days that were,
I find my lost youth again.
And the strange and beautiful song,
The groves are repeating it still:
"A boy's will is the wind's will,
And the thoughts of youth are long, long thoughts."

THE ROPEWALK

In that building, long and low,
With its windows all a-row,
Like the port-holes of a hulk,
Human spiders spin and spin,
Backward down their threads so thin
Dropping, each a hempen bulk.

At the end, an open door;
Squares of sunshine on the floor
Light the long and dusky lane;
And the whirring of a wheel,
Dull and drowsy, makes me feel
All its spokes are in my brain.

As the spinners to the end
Downward go and reascend,
Gleam the long threads in the sun;
While within this brain of mine
Cobwebs brighter and more fine
By the busy wheel are spun.

Two fair maidens in a swing,
Like white doves upon the wing,
First before my vision pass;
Laughing, as their gentle hands
Closely clasp the twisted strands,
At their shadow on the grass.

Then a booth of mountebanks,
With its smell of tan and planks,
And a girl poised high in air
On a cord, in spangled dress,
With a faded loveliness,
And a weary look of care.

Then a homestead among farms,
And a woman with bare arms
Drawing water from a well;
As the bucket mounts apace,
With it mounts her own fair face,
As at some magician's spell.

Then an old man in a tower,
Ringing loud the noontide hour,
While the rope coils round and round
Like a serpent at his feet,
And again, in swift retreat,
Nearly lifts him from the ground.

Then within a prison-yard,
Faces fixed, and stern, and hard,
Laughter and indecent mirth;
Ah! it is the gallows-tree!
Breath of Christian charity,
Blow, and sweep it from the earth!

Then a school-boy, with his kite
Gleaming in a sky of light,
And an eager, upward look;
Steeds pursued through lane and field;
Fowlers with their snares concealed;

And an angler by a brook.

Ships rejoicing in the breeze,
Wrecks that float o'er unknown seas,
Anchors dragged through faithless sand;
Sea-fog drifting overhead,
And, with lessening line and lead,
Sailors feeling for the land.

All these scenes do I behold,
These, and many left untold,
In that building long and low;
While the wheel goes round and round,
With a drowsy, dreamy sound,
And the spinners backward go.

THE GOLDEN MILE-STONE

Leafless are the trees; their purple branches
Spread themselves abroad, like reefs of coral,
Rising silent
In the Red Sea of the Winter sunset.

From the hundred chimneys of the village,
Like the Afreet in the Arabian story,
Smoky columns
Tower aloft into the air of amber.

At the window winks the flickering fire-light;
Here and there the lamps of evening glimmer,
Social watch-fires
Answering one another through the darkness.

On the hearth the lighted logs are glowing,
And like Ariel in the cloven pine-tree
For its freedom
Groans and sighs the air imprisoned in them.

By the fireside there are old men seated,
Seeing ruined cities in the ashes,
Asking sadly
Of the Past what it can ne'er restore them.

By the fireside there are youthful dreamers,
Building castles fair, with stately stairways,
Asking blindly

Of the Future what it cannot give them.

By the fireside tragedies are acted
In whose scenes appear two actors only,
Wife and husband,
And above them God the sole spectator.

By the fireside there are peace and comfort,
Wives and children, with fair, thoughtful faces,
Waiting, watching
For a well-known footstep in the passage.

Each man's chimney is his Golden Mile-stone;
Is the central point, from which he measures
Every distance
Through the gateways of the world around him.

In his farthest wanderings still he sees it;
Hears the talking flame, the answering night-wind,
As he heard them
When he sat with those who were, but are not.

Happy he whom neither wealth nor fashion,
Nor the march of the encroaching city,
Drives an exile
From the hearth of his ancestral homestead.

We may build more splendid habitations,
Fill our rooms with paintings and with sculptures,
But we cannot
Buy with gold the old associations!

CATAWBA WINE

This song of mine
Is a Song of the Vine,
To be sung by the glowing embers
Of wayside inns,
When the rain begins
To darken the drear Novembers.

It is not a song
Of the Scuppernong,
From warm Carolinian valleys,
Nor the Isabel
And the Muscadel

That bask in our garden alleys.

Nor the red Mustang,
Whose clusters hang
O'er the waves of the Colorado,
And the fiery flood
Of whose purple blood
Has a dash of Spanish bravado.

For richest and best
Is the wine of the West,
That grows by the Beautiful River;
Whose sweet perfume
Fills all the room
With a benison on the giver.

And as hollow trees
Are the haunts of bees,
For ever going and coming;
So this crystal hive
Is all alive
With a swarming and buzzing and humming.

Very good in its way
Is the Verzenay,
Or the Sillery soft and creamy;
But Catawba wine
Has a taste more divine,
More dulcet, delicious, and dreamy.

There grows no vine
By the haunted Rhine,
By Danube or Guadalquivir,
Nor on island or cape,
That bears such a grape
As grows by the Beautiful River.

Drugged is their juice
For foreign use,
When shipped o'er the reeling Atlantic,
To rack our brains
With the fever pains,
That have driven the Old World frantic.

To the sewers and sinks
With all such drinks,
And after them tumble the mixer;
For a poison malign

Is such Borgia wine,
Or at best but a Devil's Elixir.

While pure as a spring
Is the wine I sing,
And to praise it, one needs but name it;
For Catawba wine
Has need of no sign,
No tavern-bush to proclaim it.

And this Song of the Vine,
This greeting of mine,
The winds and the birds shall deliver
To the Queen of the West,
In her garlands dressed,
On the banks of the Beautiful River.

SANTA FILOMENA

Whene'er a noble deed is wrought,
Whene'er is spoken a noble thought,
Our hearts, in glad surprise,
To higher levels rise.

The tidal wave of deeper souls
Into our inmost being rolls,
And lifts us unawares
Out of all meaner cares.

Honor to those whose words or deeds
Thus help us in our daily needs,
And by their overflow
Raise us from what is low!

Thus thought I, as by night I read
Of the great army of the dead,
The trenches cold and damp,
The starved and frozen camp,--

The wounded from the battle-plain,
In dreary hospitals of pain,
The cheerless corridors,
The cold and stony floors.

Lo! in that house of misery
A lady with a lamp I see

Pass through the glimmering gloom,
And flit from room to room.

And slow, as in a dream of bliss,
The speechless sufferer turns to kiss
Her shadow, as it falls
Upon the darkening walls.

As if a door in heaven should be
Opened and then closed suddenly,
The vision came and went,
The light shone and was spent.

On England's annals, through the long
Hereafter of her speech and song,
That light its rays shall cast
From portals of the past.

A Lady with a Lamp shall stand
In the great history of the land,
A noble type of good,
Heroic womanhood.

Nor even shall be wanting here
The palm, the lily, and the spear,
The symbols that of yore
Saint Filomena bore.

THE DISCOVERER OF THE NORTH CAPE

A LEAF FROM KING ALFRED'S OROSIUS

Othere, the old sea-captain,
Who dwelt in Helgoland,
To King Alfred, the Lover of Truth,
Brought a snow-white walrus-tooth,
Which he held in his brown right hand.

His figure was tall and stately,
Like a boy's his eye appeared;
His hair was yellow as hay,
But threads of a silvery gray
Gleamed in his tawny beard.

Hearty and hale was Othere,
His cheek had the color of oak;

With a kind of laugh in his speech,
Like the sea-tide on a beach,
As unto the King he spoke.

And Alfred, King of the Saxons,
Had a book upon his knees,
And wrote down the wondrous tale
Of him who was first to sail
Into the Arctic seas.

"So far I live to the northward,
No man lives north of me;
To the east are wild mountain-chains;
And beyond them meres and plains;
To the westward all is sea.

"So far I live to the northward,
From the harbor of Skeringes-hale,
If you only sailed by day,
With a fair wind all the way,
More than a month would you sail.

"I own six hundred reindeer,
With sheep and swine beside;
I have tribute from the Finns,
Whalebone and reindeer-skins,
And ropes of walrus-hide.

"I ploughed the land with horses,
But my heart was ill at ease,
For the old seafaring men
Came to me now and then,
With their sagas of the seas;--

"Of Iceland and of Greenland,
And the stormy Hebrides,
And the undiscovered deep;--
I could not eat nor sleep
For thinking of those seas.

"To the northward stretched the desert,
How far I fain would know;
So at last I sallied forth,
And three days sailed due north,
As far as the whale-ships go.

"To the west of me was the ocean,
To the right the desolate shore,

But I did not slacken sail
For the walrus or the whale,
Till after three days more.

"The days grew longer and longer,
Till they became as one,
And southward through the haze
I saw the sullen blaze
Of the red midnight sun.

"And then uprose before me,
Upon the water's edge,
The huge and haggard shape
Of that unknown North Cape,
Whose form is like a wedge.

"The sea was rough and stormy,
The tempest howled and wailed,
And the sea-fog, like a ghost,
Haunted that dreary coast,
But onward still I sailed.

"Four days I steered to eastward,
Four days without a night:
Round in a fiery ring
Went the great sun, O King,
With red and lurid light."

Here Alfred, King of the Saxons,
Ceased writing for a while;
And raised his eyes from his book,
With a strange and puzzled look,
And an incredulous smile.

But Othere, the old sea-captain,
He neither paused nor stirred,
Till the King listened, and then
Once more took up his pen,
And wrote down every word.

"And now the land," said Othere,
"Bent southward suddenly,
And I followed the curving shore
And ever southward bore
Into a nameless sea.

"And there we hunted the walrus,
The narwhale, and the seal;

Ha! 't was a noble game!
And like the lightning's flame
Flew our harpoons of steel.

"There were six of us all together,
Norsemen of Helgoland;
In two days and no more
We killed of them threescore,
And dragged them to the strand!"

Here Alfred the Truth-Teller
Suddenly closed his book,
And lifted his blue eyes,
With doubt and strange surmise
Depicted in their look.

And Othere the old sea-captain
Stared at him wild and weird,
Then smiled, till his shining teeth
Gleamed white from underneath
His tawny, quivering beard.

And to the King of the Saxons,
In witness of the truth,
Raising his noble head,
He stretched his brown hand, and said,
"Behold this walrus-tooth!"

DAYBREAK

A wind came up out of the sea,
And said, "O mists, make room for me."

It hailed the ships, and cried, "Sail on,
Ye mariners, the night is gone."

And hurried landward far away,
Crying, "Awake! it is the day."

It said unto the forest, "Shout!
Hang all your leafy banners out!"

It touched the wood-bird's folded wing,
And said, "O bird, awake and sing."

And o'er the farms, "O chanticleer,

Your clarion blow; the day is near."

It whispered to the fields of corn,
"Bow down, and hail the coming morn."

It shouted through the belfry-tower,
"Awake, O bell! proclaim the hour."

It crossed the churchyard with a sigh,
And said, "Not yet! in quiet lie."

THE FIFTIETH BIRTHDAY OF AGASSIZ

MAY 28, 1857

It was fifty years ago
In the pleasant month of May,
In the beautiful Pays de Vaud,
A child in its cradle lay.

And Nature, the old nurse, took
The child upon her knee,
Saying: "Here is a story-book
Thy Father has written for thee."

"Come, wander with me," she said,
"Into regions yet untrod;
And read what is still unread
In the manuscripts of God."

And he wandered away and away
With Nature, the dear old nurse,
Who sang to him night and day
The rhymes of the universe.

And whenever the way seemed long,
Or his heart began to fail,
She would sing a more wonderful song,
Or tell a more marvellous tale.

So she keeps him still a child,
And will not let him go,
Though at times his heart beats wild
For the beautiful Pays de Vaud;

Though at times he hears in his dreams

The Ranz des Vaches of old,
And the rush of mountain streams
From glaciers clear and cold;

And the mother at home says, "Hark!
For his voice I listen and yearn;
It is growing late and dark,
And my boy does not return!"

CHILDREN

Come to me, O ye children!
For I hear you at your play,
And the questions that perplexed me
Have vanished quite away.

Ye open the eastern windows,
That look towards the sun,
Where thoughts are singing swallows
And the brooks of morning run.

In your hearts are the birds and the sunshine,
In your thoughts the brooklet's flow,
But in mine is the wind of Autumn
And the first fall of the snow.

Ah! what would the world be to us
If the children were no more?
We should dread the desert behind us
Worse than the dark before.

What the leaves are to the forest,
With light and air for food,
Ere their sweet and tender juices
Have been hardened into wood,--

That to the world are children;
Through them it feels the glow
Of a brighter and sunnier climate
Than reaches the trunks below.

Come to me, O ye children!
And whisper in my ear
What the birds and the winds are singing
In your sunny atmosphere.

For what are all our contrivings,
And the wisdom of our books,
When compared with your caresses,
And the gladness of your looks?

Ye are better than all the ballads
That ever were sung or said;
For ye are living poems,
And all the rest are dead.

SANDALPHON

Have you read in the Talmud of old,
In the Legends the Rabbins have told
Of the limitless realms of the air,--
Have you read it,--the marvellous story
Of Sandalphon, the Angel of Glory,
Sandalphon, the Angel of Prayer?

How, erect, at the outermost gates
Of the City Celestial he waits,
With his feet on the ladder of light,
That, crowded with angels unnumbered,
By Jacob was seen, as he slumbered
Alone in the desert at night?

The Angels of Wind and of Fire
Chant only one hymn, and expire
With the song's irresistible stress;
Expire in their rapture and wonder,
As harp-strings are broken asunder
By music they throb to express.

But serene in the rapturous throng,
Unmoved by the rush of the song,
With eyes unimpassioned and slow,
Among the dead angels, the deathless
Sandalphon stands listening breathless
To sounds that ascend from below;--

From the spirits on earth that adore,
From the souls that entreat and implore
In the fervor and passion of prayer;
From the hearts that are broken with losses,
And weary with dragging the crosses
Too heavy for mortals to bear.

And he gathers the prayers as he stands,
And they change into flowers in his hands,
Into garlands of purple and red;
And beneath the great arch of the portal,
Through the streets of the City Immortal
Is wafted the fragrance they shed.

It is but a legend, I know,--
A fable, a phantom, a show,
Of the ancient Rabbinical lore;
Yet the old mediaeval tradition,
The beautiful, strange superstition,
But haunts me and holds me the more.

When I look from my window at night,
And the welkin above is all white,
All throbbing and panting with stars,
Among them majestic is standing
Sandalphon the angel, expanding
His pinions in nebulous bars.

And the legend, I feel, is a part
Of the hunger and thirst of the heart,
The frenzy and fire of the brain,
That grasps at the fruitage forbidden,
The golden pomegranates of Eden,
To quiet its fever and pain.

FLIGHT THE SECOND

THE CHILDREN'S HOUR

Between the dark and the daylight,
When the night is beginning to lower,
Comes a pause in the day's occupations,
That is known as the Children's Hour.

I hear in the chamber above me
The patter of little feet,
The sound of a door that is opened,
And voices soft and sweet.

From my study I see in the lamplight,
Descending the broad hall stair,
Grave Alice, and laughing Allegra,

And Edith with golden hair.

A whisper, and then a silence:
Yet I know by their merry eyes
They are plotting and planning together
To take me by surprise.

A sudden rush from the stairway,
A sudden raid from the hall!
By three doors left unguarded
They enter my castle wall!

They climb up into my turret
O'er the arms and back of my chair;
If I try to escape, they surround me;
They seem to be everywhere.

They almost devour me with kisses,
Their arms about me entwine,
Till I think of the Bishop of Bingen
In his Mouse-Tower on the Rhine!

Do you think, o blue-eyed banditti,
Because you have scaled the wall,
Such an old mustache as I am
Is not a match for you all!

I have you fast in my fortress,
And will not let you depart,
But put you down into the dungeon
In the round-tower of my heart.

And there will I keep you forever,
Yes, forever and a day,
Till the walls shall crumble to ruin,
And moulder in dust away!

ENCELADUS

Under Mount Etna he lies,
It is slumber, it is not death;
For he struggles at times to arise,
And above him the lurid skies
Are hot with his fiery breath.

The crags are piled on his breast,

The earth is heaped on his head;
But the groans of his wild unrest,
Though smothered and half suppressed,
Are heard, and he is not dead.

And the nations far away
Are watching with eager eyes;
They talk together and say,
"To-morrow, perhaps to-day,
Euceladus will arise!"

And the old gods, the austere
Oppressors in their strength,
Stand aghast and white with fear
At the ominous sounds they hear,
And tremble, and mutter, "At length!"

Ah me! for the land that is sown
With the harvest of despair!
Where the burning cinders, blown
From the lips of the overthrown
Enceladus, fill the air.

Where ashes are heaped in drifts
Over vineyard and field and town,
Whenever he starts and lifts
His head through the blackened rifts
Of the crags that keep him down.

See, see! the red light shines!
'T is the glare of his awful eyes!
And the storm-wind shouts through the pines
Of Alps and of Apennines,
"Enceladus, arise!"

THE CUMBERLAND

At anchor in Hampton Roads we lay,
On board of the cumberland, sloop-of-war;
And at times from the fortress across the bay
The alarum of drums swept past,
Or a bugle blast
From the camp on the shore.

Then far away to the south uprose
A little feather of snow-white smoke,

And we knew that the iron ship of our foes
Was steadily steering its course
To try the force
Of our ribs of oak.

Down upon us heavily runs,
Silent and sullen, the floating fort;
Then comes a puff of smoke from her guns,
And leaps the terrible death,
With fiery breath,
From each open port.

We are not idle, but send her straight
Defiance back in a full broadside!
As hail rebounds from a roof of slate,
Rebounds our heavier hail
From each iron scale
Of the monster's hide.

"Strike your flag!" the rebel cries,
In his arrogant old plantation strain.
"Never!" our gallant Morris replies;
"It is better to sink than to yield!"
And the whole air pealed
With the cheers of our men.

Then, like a kraken huge and black,
She crushed our ribs in her iron grasp!
Down went the Cumberland all a wrack,
With a sudden shudder of death,
And the cannon's breath
For her dying gasp.

Next morn, as the sun rose over the bay,
Still floated our flag at the mainmast head.
Lord, how beautiful was Thy day!
Every waft of the air
Was a whisper of prayer,
Or a dirge for the dead.

Ho! brave hearts that went down in the seas
Ye are at peace in the troubled stream;
Ho! brave land! with hearts like these,
Thy flag, that is rent in twain,
Shall be one again,
And without a seam!

SNOW-FLAKES

Out of the bosom of the Air,
Out of the cloud-folds of her garments shaken,
Over the woodlands brown and bare,
Over the harvest-fields forsaken,
Silent, and soft, and slow
Descends the snow.

Even as our cloudy fancies take
Suddenly shape in some divine expression,
Even as the troubled heart doth make
In the white countenance confession,
The troubled sky reveals
The grief it feels.

This is the poem of the air,
Slowly in silent syllables recorded;
This is the secret of despair,
Long in its cloudy bosom hoarded,
Now whispered and revealed
To wood and field.

A DAY OF SUNSHINE

O gift of God! O perfect day:
Whereon shall no man work, but play;
Whereon it is enough for me,
Not to be doing, but to be!

Through every fibre of my brain,
Through every nerve, through every vein,
I feel the electric thrill, the touch
Of life, that seems almost too much.

I hear the wind among the trees
Playing celestial symphonies;
I see the branches downward bent,
Like keys of some great instrument.

And over me unrolls on high
The splendid scenery of the sky,
Where though a sapphire sea the sun
Sails like a golden galleon,

Towards yonder cloud-land in the West,
Towards yonder Islands of the Blest,
Whose steep sierra far uplifts
Its craggy summits white with drifts.

Blow, winds! and waft through all the rooms
The snow-flakes of the cherry-blooms!
Blow, winds! and bend within my reach
The fiery blossoms of the peach!

O Life and Love! O happy throng
Of thoughts, whose only speech is song!
O heart of man! canst thou not be
Blithe as the air is, and as free?

SOMETHING LEFT UNDONE

Labor with what zeal we will,
Something still remains undone,
Something uncompleted still
Waits the rising of the sun.

By the bedside, on the stair,
At the threshold, near the gates,
With its menace or its prayer,
Like a mendicant it waits;

Waits, and will not go away;
Waits, and will not be gainsaid;
By the cares of yesterday
Each to-day is heavier made;

Till at length the burden seems
Greater than our strength can bear,
Heavy as the weight of dreams,
Pressing on us everywhere.

And we stand from day to day,
Like the dwarfs of times gone by,
Who, as Northern legends say,
On their shoulders held the sky.

WEARINESS

O little feet! that such long years
Must wander on through hopes and fears,
Must ache and bleed beneath your load;
I, nearer to the wayside inn
Where toil shall cease and rest begin,
Am weary, thinking of your road!

O little hands! that, weak or strong,
Have still to serve or rule so long,
Have still so long to give or ask;
I, who so much with book and pen
Have toiled among my fellow-men,
Am weary, thinking of your task.

O little hearts! that throb and beat
With such impatient, feverish heat,
Such limitless and strong desires;
Mine that so long has glowed and burned,
With passions into ashes turned
Now covers and conceals its fires.

O little souls! as pure and white
And crystalline as rays of light
Direct from heaven, their source divine;
Refracted through the mist of years,
How red my setting sun appears,
How lurid looks this soul of mine!

FLIGHT THE THIRD

FATA MORGANA

O sweet illusions of Song,
That tempt me everywhere,
In the lonely fields, and the throng
Of the crowded thoroughfare!

I approach, and ye vanish away,
I grasp you, and ye are gone;
But ever by nigh an day,
The melody soundeth on.

As the weary traveller sees
In desert or prairie vast,
Blue lakes, overhung with trees,
That a pleasant shadow cast;

Fair towns with turrets high,
And shining roofs of gold,
That vanish as he draws nigh,
Like mists together rolled,--

So I wander and wander along,
And forever before me gleams
The shining city of song,
In the beautiful land of dreams.

But when I would enter the gate
Of that golden atmosphere,
It is gone, and I wander and wait
For the vision to reappear.

THE HAUNTED CHAMBER

Each heart has its haunted chamber,
Where the silent moonlight falls!
On the floor are mysterious footsteps,
There are whispers along the walls!

And mine at times is haunted
By phantoms of the Past
As motionless as shadows
By the silent moonlight cast.

A form sits by the window,
That is not seen by day,
For as soon as the dawn approaches
It vanishes away.

It sits there in the moonlight
Itself as pale and still,
And points with its airy finger
Across the window-sill.

Without before the window,
There stands a gloomy pine,
Whose boughs wave upward and downward
As wave these thoughts of mine.

And underneath its branches
Is the grave of a little child,
Who died upon life's threshold,

And never wept nor smiled.

What are ye, O pallid phantoms!
That haunt my troubled brain?
That vanish when day approaches,
And at night return again?

What are ye, O pallid phantoms!
But the statues without breath,
That stand on the bridge overarching
The silent river of death?

THE MEETING

After so long an absence
At last we meet again:
Does the meeting give us pleasure,
Or does it give us pain?

The tree of life has been shaken,
And but few of us linger now,
Like the Prophet's two or three berries
In the top of the uppermost bough.

We cordially greet each other
In the old, familiar tone;
And we think, though we do not say it,
How old and gray he is grown!

We speak of a Merry Christmas
And many a Happy New Year
But each in his heart is thinking
Of those that are not here.

We speak of friends and their fortunes,
And of what they did and said,
Till the dead alone seem living,
And the living alone seem dead.

And at last we hardly distinguish
Between the ghosts and the guests;
And a mist and shadow of sadness
Steals over our merriest jests.

VOX POPULI

When Mazarvan the Magician,
Journeyed westward through Cathay,
Nothing heard he but the praises
Of Badoura on his way.

But the lessening rumor ended
When he came to Khaledan,
There the folk were talking only
Of Prince Camaralzaman,

So it happens with the poets:
Every province hath its own;
Camaralzaman is famous
Where Badoura is unknown.

THE CASTLE-BUILDER

A gentle boy, with soft and silken locks
A dreamy boy, with brown and tender eyes,
A castle-builder, with his wooden blocks,
And towers that touch imaginary skies.

A fearless rider on his father's knee,
An eager listener unto stories told
At the Round Table of the nursery,
Of heroes and adventures manifold.

There will be other towers for thee to build;
There will be other steeds for thee to ride;
There will be other legends, and all filled
With greater marvels and more glorified.

Build on, and make thy castles high and fair,
Rising and reaching upward to the skies;
Listen to voices in the upper air,
Nor lose thy simple faith in mysteries.

CHANGED

From the outskirts of the town
Where of old the mile-stone stood.
Now a stranger, looking down

I behold the shadowy crown
Of the dark and haunted wood.

Is it changed, or am I changed?
Ah! the oaks are fresh and green,
But the friends with whom I ranged
Through their thickets are estranged
By the years that intervene.

Bright as ever flows the sea,
Bright as ever shines the sun,
But alas! they seem to me
Not the sun that used to be,
Not the tides that used to run.

THE CHALLENGE

I have a vague remembrance
Of a story, that is told
In some ancient Spanish legend
Or chronicle of old.

It was when brave King Sanchez
Was before Zamora slain,
And his great besieging army
Lay encamped upon the plain.

Don Diego de Ordonez
Sallied forth in front of all,
And shouted loud his challenge
To the warders on the wall.

All the people of Zamora,
Both the born and the unborn,
As traitors did he challenge
With taunting words of scorn.

The living, in their houses,
And in their graves, the dead!
And the waters of their rivers,
And their wine, and oil, and bread!

There is a greater army,
That besets us round with strife,
A starving, numberless army,
At all the gates of life.

The poverty-stricken millions
Who challenge our wine and bread,
And impeach us all as traitors,
Both the living and the dead.

And whenever I sit at the banquet,
Where the feast and song are high,
Amid the mirth and the music
I can hear that fearful cry.

And hollow and haggard faces
Look into the lighted hall,
And wasted hands are extended
To catch the crumbs that fall.

For within there is light and plenty,
And odors fill the air;
But without there is cold and darkness,
And hunger and despair.

And there in the camp of famine,
In wind and cold and rain,
Christ, the great Lord of the army,
Lies dead upon the plain!

THE BROOK AND THE WAVE

The brooklet came from the mountain,
As sang the bard of old,
Running with feet of silver
Over the sands of gold!

Far away in the briny ocean
There rolled a turbulent wave,
Now singing along the sea-beach,
Now howling along the cave.

And the brooklet has found the billow
Though they flowed so far apart,
And has filled with its freshness and sweetness
That turbulent bitter heart!

AFTERMATH

When the summer fields are mown,
When the birds are fledged and flown,
And the dry leaves strew the path;
With the falling of the snow,
With the cawing of the crow,
Once again the fields we mow
And gather in the aftermath.

Not the sweet, new grass with flowers
Is this harvesting of ours;
Not the upland clover bloom;
But the rowen mired with weeds,
Tangled tufts from marsh and meads,
Where the poppy drops its seeds
In the silence and the gloom.

FLIGHT THE FOURTH

CHARLES SUMNER

Garlands upon his grave,
And flowers upon his hearse,
And to the tender heart and brave
The tribute of this verse.

His was the troubled life,
The conflict and the pain,
The grief, the bitterness of strife,
The honor without stain.

Like Winkelried, he took
Into his manly breast
The sheaf of hostile spears, and broke
A path for the oppressed.

Then from the fatal field
Upon a nation's heart
Borne like a warrior on his shield!--
So should the brave depart.

Death takes us by surprise,
And stays our hurrying feet;
The great design unfinished lies,
Our lives are incomplete.

But in the dark unknown
Perfect their circles seem,
Even as a bridge's arch of stone
Is rounded in the stream.

Alike are life and death,
When life in death survives,
And the uninterrupted breath
Inspires a thousand lives.

Were a star quenched on high,
For ages would its light,
Still travelling downward from the sky,
Shine on our mortal sight.

So when a great man dies,
For years beyond our ken,
The light he leaves behind him lies
Upon the paths of men.

TRAVELS BY THE FIRESIDE

The ceaseless rain is falling fast,
And yonder gilded vane,
Immovable for three days past,
Points to the misty main,

It drives me in upon myself
And to the fireside gleams,
To pleasant books that crowd my shelf,
And still more pleasant dreams,

I read whatever bards have sung
Of lands beyond the sea,
And the bright days when I was young
Come thronging back to me.

In fancy I can hear again
The Alpine torrent's roar,
The mule-bells on the hills of Spain,
The sea at Elsinore.

I see the convent's gleaming wall
Rise from its groves of pine,
And towers of old cathedrals tall,
And castles by the Rhine.

I journey on by park and spire,
Beneath centennial trees,
Through fields with poppies all on fire,
And gleams of distant seas.

I fear no more the dust and heat,
No more I feel fatigue,
While journeying with another's feet
O'er many a lengthening league.

Let others traverse sea and land,
And toil through various climes,
I turn the world round with my hand
Reading these poets' rhymes.

From them I learn whatever lies
Beneath each changing zone,
And see, when looking with their eyes,
Better than with mine own.

CADENABBIA

LAKE OF COMO

No sound of wheels or hoof-beat breaks
The silence of the summer day,
As by the loveliest of all lakes
I while the idle hours away.

I pace the leafy colonnade
Where level branches of the plane
Above me weave a roof of shade
Impervious to the sun and rain.

At times a sudden rush of air
Flutters the lazy leaves o'erhead,
And gleams of sunshine toss and flare
Like torches down the path I tread.

By Somariva's garden gate
I make the marble stairs my seat,
And hear the water, as I wait,
Lapping the steps beneath my feet.

The undulation sinks and swells

Along the stony parapets,
And far away the floating bells
Tinkle upon the fisher's nets.

Silent and slow, by tower and town
The freighted barges come and go,
Their pendent shadows gliding down
By town and tower submerged below.

The hills sweep upward from the shore,
With villas scattered one by one
Upon their wooded spurs, and lower
Bellaggio blazing in the sun.

And dimly seen, a tangled mass
Of walls and woods, of light and shade,
Stands beckoning up the Stelvio Pass
Varenna with its white cascade.

I ask myself, Is this a dream?
Will it all vanish into air?
Is there a land of such supreme
And perfect beauty anywhere?

Sweet vision! Do not fade away;
Linger until my heart shall take
Into itself the summer day,
And all the beauty of the lake.

Linger until upon my brain
Is stamped an image of the scene,
Then fade into the air again,
And be as if thou hadst not been.

MONTE CASSINO

TERRA DI LAVORO

Beautiful valley! through whose verdant meads
Unheard the Garigliano glides along;--
The Liris, nurse of rushes and of reeds,
The river taciturn of classic song.

The Land of Labor and the Land of Rest,
Where mediaeval towns are white on all
The hillsides, and where every mountain's crest

Is an Etrurian or a Roman wall.

There is Alagna, where Pope Boniface
Was dragged with contumely from his throne;
Sciarra Colonna, was that day's disgrace
The Pontiff's only, or in part thine own?

There is Ceprano, where a renegade
Was each Apulian, as great Dante saith,
When Manfred by his men-at-arms betrayed
Spurred on to Benevento and to death.

There is Aquinum, the old Volscian town,
Where Juvenal was born, whose lurid light
Still hovers o'er his birthplace like the crown
Of splendor seen o'er cities in the night.

Doubled the splendor is, that in its streets
The Angelic Doctor as a school-boy played,
And dreamed perhaps the dreams, that he repeats
In ponderous folios for scholastics made.

And there, uplifted, like a passing cloud
That pauses on a mountain summit high,
Monte Cassino's convent rears its proud
And venerable walls against the sky.

Well I remember how on foot I climbed
The stony pathway leading to its gate;
Above, the convent bells for vespers chimed,
Below, the darkening town grew desolate.

Well I remember the low arch and dark,
The court-yard with its well, the terrace wide,
From which, far down, the valley like a park
Veiled in the evening mists, was dim descried.

The day was dying, and with feeble hands
Caressed the mountain-tops; the vales between
Darkened; the river in the meadowlands
Sheathed itself as a sword, and was not seen.

The silence of the place was like a sleep,
So full of rest it seemed; each passing tread
Was a reverberation from the deep
Recesses of the ages that are dead.

For, more than thirteen centuries ago,

Benedict fleeing from the gates of Rome,
A youth disgusted with its vice and woe,
Sought in these mountain solitudes a home.

He founded here his Convent and his Rule
Of prayer and work, and counted work as prayer;
The pen became a clarion, and his school
Flamed like a beacon in the midnight air.

What though Boccaccio, in his reckless way,
Mocking the lazy brotherhood, deplores
The illuminated manuscripts, that lay
Torn and neglected on the dusty floors?

Boccaccio was a novelist, a child
Of fancy and of fiction at the best!
This the urbane librarian said, and smiled
Incredulous, as at some idle jest.

Upon such themes as these, with one young friar
I sat conversing late into the night,
Till in its cavernous chimney the woodfire
Had burnt its heart out like an anchorite.

And then translated, in my convent cell,
Myself yet not myself, in dreams I lay,
And, as a monk who hears the matin bell,
Started from sleep; already it was day.

From the high window I beheld the scene
On which Saint Benedict so oft had gazed,--
The mountains and the valley in the sheen
Of the bright sun,--and stood as one amazed.

Gray mists were rolling, rising, vanishing;
The woodlands glistened with their jewelled crowns;
Far off the mellow bells began to ring
For matins in the half-awakened towns.

The conflict of the Present and the Past,
The ideal and the actual in our life,
As on a field of battle held me fast,
Where this world and the next world were at strife.

For, as the valley from its sleep awoke,
I saw the iron horses of the steam
Toss to the morning air their plumes of smoke,
And woke, as one awaketh from a dream.

AMALFI

Sweet the memory is to me
Of a land beyond the sea,
Where the waves and mountains meet,
Where, amid her mulberry-trees
Sits Amalfi in the heat,
Bathing ever her white feet
In the tideless summer seas.

In the middle of the town,
From its fountains in the hills,
Tumbling through the narrow gorge,
The Canneto rushes down,
Turns the great wheels of the mills,
Lifts the hammers of the forge.

'T is a stairway, not a street,
That ascends the deep ravine,
Where the torrent leaps between
Rocky walls that almost meet.
Toiling up from stair to stair
Peasant girls their burdens bear;
Sunburnt daughters of the soil,
Stately figures tall and straight,
What inexorable fate
Dooms them to this life of toil?

Lord of vineyards and of lands,
Far above the convent stands.
On its terraced walk aloof
Leans a monk with folded hands,
Placid, satisfied, serene,
Looking down upon the scene
Over wall and red-tiled roof;
Wondering unto what good end
All this toil and traffic tend,
And why all men cannot be
Free from care and free from pain,
And the sordid love of gain,
And as indolent as he.

Where are now the freighted barks
From the marts of east and west?
Where the knights in iron sarks

Journeying to the Holy Land,
Glove of steel upon the hand,
Cross of crimson on the breast?
Where the pomp of camp and court?
Where the pilgrims with their prayers?
Where the merchants with their wares,
And their gallant brigantines
Sailing safely into port
Chased by corsair Algerines?

Vanished like a fleet of cloud,
Like a passing trumpet-blast,
Are those splendors of the past,
And the commerce and the crowd!
Fathoms deep beneath the seas
Lie the ancient wharves and quays,
Swallowed by the engulfing waves;
Silent streets and vacant halls,
Ruined roofs and towers and walls;
Hidden from all mortal eyes
Deep the sunken city lies:
Even cities have their graves!

This is an enchanted land!
Round the headlands far away
Sweeps the blue Salernian bay
With its sickle of white sand:
Further still and furthermost
On the dim discovered coast
Paestum with its ruins lies,
And its roses all in bloom
Seem to tinge the fatal skies
Of that lonely land of doom.

On his terrace, high in air,
Nothing doth the good monk care
For such worldly themes as these,
From the garden just below
Little puffs of perfume blow,
And a sound is in his ears
Of the murmur of the bees
In the shining chestnut-trees;
Nothing else he heeds or hears.
All the landscape seems to swoon
In the happy afternoon;
Slowly o'er his senses creep
The encroaching waves of sleep,
And he sinks as sank the town,

Unresisting, fathoms down,
Into caverns cool and deep!

Walled about with drifts of snow,
Hearing the fierce north-wind blow,
Seeing all the landscape white,
And the river cased in ice,
Comes this memory of delight,
Comes this vision unto me
Of a long-lost Paradise
In the land beyond the sea.

THE SERMON OF ST. FRANCIS

Up soared the lark into the air,
A shaft of song, a winged prayer,
As if a soul, released from pain,
Were flying back to heaven again.

St. Francis heard; it was to him
An emblem of the Seraphim;
The upward motion of the fire,
The light, the heat, the heart's desire.

Around Assisi's convent gate
The birds, God's poor who cannot wait,
From moor and mere and darksome wood
Came flocking for their dole of food.

"O brother birds," St. Francis said,
"Ye come to me and ask for bread,
But not with bread alone to-day
Shall ye be fed and sent away.

"Ye shall be fed, ye happy birds,
With manna of celestial words;
Not mine, though mine they seem to be,
Not mine, though they be spoken through me.

"O, doubly are ye bound to praise
The great Creator in your lays;
He giveth you your plumes of down,
Your crimson hoods, your cloaks of brown.

"He giveth you your wings to fly
And breathe a purer air on high,

And careth for you everywhere,
Who for yourselves so little care!"

With flutter of swift wings and songs
Together rose the feathered throngs,
And singing scattered far apart;
Deep peace was in St. Francis' heart.

He knew not if the brotherhood
His homily had understood;
He only knew that to one ear
The meaning of his words was clear.

BELISARIUS

I am poor and old and blind;
The sun burns me, and the wind
Blows through the city gate
And covers me with dust
From the wheels of the august
Justinian the Great.

It was for him I chased
The Persians o'er wild and waste,
As General of the East;
Night after night I lay
In their camps of yesterday;
Their forage was my feast.

For him, with sails of red,
And torches at mast-head,
Piloting the great fleet,
I swept the Afric coasts
And scattered the Vandal hosts,
Like dust in a windy street.

For him I won again
The Ausonian realm and reign,
Rome and Parthenope;
And all the land was mine
From the summits of Apennine
To the shores of either sea.

For him, in my feeble age,
I dared the battle's rage,
To save Byzantium's state,

When the tents of Zabergan,
Like snow-drifts overran
The road to the Golden Gate.

And for this, for this, behold!
Infirm and blind and old,
With gray, uncovered head,
Beneath the very arch
Of my triumphal march,
I stand and beg my bread!

Methinks I still can hear,
Sounding distinct and near,
The Vandal monarch's cry,
As, captive and disgraced,
With majestic step he paced,--
"All, all is Vanity!"

Ah! vainest of all things
Is the gratitude of kings;
The plaudits of the crowd
Are but the clatter of feet
At midnight in the street,
Hollow and restless and loud.

But the bitterest disgrace
Is to see forever the face
Of the Monk of Ephesus!
The unconquerable will
This, too, can bear;--I still
Am Belisarius!

SONGO RIVER

Nowhere such a devious stream,
Save in fancy or in dream,
Winding slow through bush and brake
Links together lake and lake.

Walled with woods or sandy shelf,
Ever doubling on itself
Flows the stream, so still and slow
That it hardly seems to flow.

Never errant knight of old,
Lost in woodland or on wold,

Such a winding path pursued
Through the sylvan solitude.

Never school-boy in his quest
After hazel-nut or nest,
Through the forest in and out
Wandered loitering thus about.

In the mirror of its tide
Tangled thickets on each side
Hang inverted, and between
Floating cloud or sky serene.

Swift or swallow on the wing
Seems the only living thing,
Or the loon, that laughs and flies
Down to those reflected skies.

Silent stream! thy Indian name
Unfamiliar is to fame;
For thou hidest here alone,
Well content to be unknown.

But thy tranquil waters teach
Wisdom deep as human speech,
Moving without haste or noise
In unbroken equipoise.

Though thou turnest no busy mill,
And art ever calm and still,
Even thy silence seems to say
To the traveller on his way:--

"Traveller, hurrying from the heat
Of the city, stay thy feet!
Rest awhile, nor longer waste
Life with inconsiderate haste!

"Be not like a stream that brawls
Loud with shallow waterfalls,
But in quiet self-control
Link together soul and soul"

FLIGHT THE FIFTH

THE HERONS OF ELMWOOD

Warm and still is the summer night,
As here by the river's brink I wander;
White overhead are the stars, and white
The glimmering lamps on the hillside yonder.

Silent are all the sounds of day;
Nothing I hear but the chirp of crickets,
And the cry of the herons winging their way
O'er the poet's house in the Elmwood thickets.

Call to him, herons, as slowly you pass
To your roosts in the haunts of the exiled thrushes,
Sing him the song of the green morass;
And the tides that water the reeds and rushes.

Sing him the mystical Song of the Hern,
And the secret that baffles our utmost seeking;
For only a sound of lament we discern,
And cannot interpret the words you are speaking.

Sing of the air, and the wild delight
Of wings that uplift and winds that uphold you,
The joy of freedom, the rapture of flight
Through the drift of the floating mists that infold you.

Of the landscape lying so far below,
With its towns and rivers and desert places;
And the splendor of light above, and the glow
Of the limitless, blue, ethereal spaces.

Ask him if songs of the Troubadours,
Or of Minnesingers in old black-letter,
Sound in his ears more sweet than yours,
And if yours are not sweeter and wilder and better.

Sing to him, say to him, here at his gate,
Where the boughs of the stately elms are meeting,
Some one hath lingered to meditate,
And send him unseen this friendly greeting;

That many another hath done the same,
Though not by a sound was the silence broken;
The surest pledge of a deathless name
Is the silent homage of thoughts unspoken.

A DUTCH PICTURE

Simon Danz has come home again,
From cruising about with his buccaneers;
He has singed the beard of the King of Spain,
And carried away the Dean of Jaen
And sold him in Algiers.

In his house by the Maese, with its roof of tiles,
And weathercocks flying aloft in air,
There are silver tankards of antique styles,
Plunder of convent and castle, and piles
Of carpets rich and rare.

In his tulip-garden there by the town,
Overlooking the sluggish stream,
With his Moorish cap and dressing-gown,
The old sea-captain, hale and brown,
Walks in a waking dream.

A smile in his gray mustachio lurks
Whenever he thinks of the King of Spain,
And the listed tulips look like Turks,
And the silent gardener as he works
Is changed to the Dean of Jaen.

The windmills on the outermost
Verge of the landscape in the haze,
To him are towers on the Spanish coast,
With whiskered sentinels at their post,
Though this is the river Maese.

But when the winter rains begin,
He sits and smokes by the blazing brands,
And old seafaring men come in,
Goat-bearded, gray, and with double chin,
And rings upon their hands.

They sit there in the shadow and shine
Of the flickering fire of the winter night;
Figures in color and design
Like those by Rembrandt of the Rhine,
Half darkness and half light.

And they talk of ventures lost or won,
And their talk is ever and ever the same,
While they drink the red wine of Tarragon,
From the cellars of some Spanish Don,

Or convent set on flame.

Restless at times with heavy strides
He paces his parlor to and fro;
He is like a ship that at anchor rides,
And swings with the rising and falling tides,
And tugs at her anchor-tow.

Voices mysterious far and near,
Sound of the wind and sound of the sea,
Are calling and whispering in his ear,
"Simon Danz! Why stayest thou here?
Come forth and follow me!"

So he thinks he shall take to the sea again
For one more cruise with his buccaneers,
To singe the beard of the King of Spain,
And capture another Dean of Jaen
And sell him in Algiers.

CASTLES IN SPAIN

How much of my young heart, O Spain,
Went out to thee in days of yore!
What dreams romantic filled my brain,
And summoned back to life again
The Paladins of Charlemagne
The Cid Campeador!

And shapes more shadowy than these,
In the dim twilight half revealed;
Phoenician galleys on the seas,
The Roman camps like hives of bees,
The Goth uplifting from his knees
Pelayo on his shield.

It was these memories perchance,
From annals of remotest eld,
That lent the colors of romance
To every trivial circumstance,
And changed the form and countenance
Of all that I beheld.

Old towns, whose history lies hid
In monkish chronicle or rhyme,
Burgos, the birthplace of the Cid,

Zamora and Valladolid,
Toledo, built and walled amid
The wars of Wamba's time;

The long, straight line of the high-way,
The distant town that seems so near,
The peasants in the fields, that stay
Their toil to cross themselves and pray,
When from the belfry at midday
The Angelus they hear;

White crosses in the mountain pass,
Mules gay with tassels, the loud din
Of muleteers, the tethered ass
That crops the dusty wayside grass,
And cavaliers with spurs of brass
Alighting at the inn;

White hamlets hidden in fields of wheat,
White cities slumbering by the sea,
White sunshine flooding square and street,
Dark mountain-ranges, at whose feet
The river-beds are dry with heat,--
All was a dream to me.

Yet something sombre and severe
O'er the enchanted landscape reigned;
A terror in the atmosphere
As if King Philip listened near,
Or Torquemada, the austere,
His ghostly sway maintained.

The softer Andalusian skies
Dispelled the sadness and the gloom;
There Cadiz by the seaside lies,
And Seville's orange-orchards rise,
Making the land a paradise
Of beauty and of bloom.

There Cordova is hidden among
The palm, the olive, and the vine;
Gem of the South, by poets sung,
And in whose Mosque Ahmanzor hung
As lamps the bells that once had rung
At Compostella's shrine.

But over all the rest supreme,
The star of stars, the cynosure,

The artist's and the poet's theme,
The young man's vision, the old man's dream,--
Granada by its winding stream,
The city of the Moor!

And there the Alhambra still recalls
Aladdin's palace of delight;
Allah il Allah! through its halls
Whispers the fountain as it falls,
The Darro darts beneath its walls,
The hills with snow are white.

Ah yes, the hills are white with snow,
And cold with blasts that bite and freeze;
But in the happy vale below
The orange and pomegranate grow,
And wafts of air toss to and fro
The blossoming almond-trees.

The Vega cleft by the Xenil,
The fascination and allure
Of the sweet landscape chains the will;
The traveller lingers on the hill,
His parted lips are breathing still
The last sigh of the Moor.

How like a ruin overgrown
With flower's that hide the rents of time,
Stands now the Past that I have known,
Castles in Spain, not built of stone
But of white summer clouds, and blown
Into this little mist of rhyme!

VITTORIA COLONNA

Vittoria Colonna, on the death of her hushand, the Marchese di Pescara, retired to her castle at Ischia (Inarime), and there wrote the Ode upon his death, which gained her the title of Divine.

Once more, once more, Inarime,
I see thy purple hills!--once more
I hear the billows of the bay
Wash the white pebbles on thy shore.

High o'er the sea-surge and the sands,
Like a great galleon wrecked and cast
Ashore by storms, thy castle stands,

A mouldering landmark of the Past.

Upon its terrace-walk I see
A phantom gliding to and fro;
It is Colonna,--it is she
Who lived and loved so long ago.

Pescara's beautiful young wife,
The type of perfect womanhood,
Whose life was love, the life of life,
That time and change and death withstood.

For death, that breaks the marriage band
In others, only closer pressed
The wedding-ring upon her hand
And closer locked and barred her breast.

She knew the life-long martyrdom,
The weariness, the endless pain
Of waiting for some one to come
Who nevermore would come again.

The shadows of the chestnut-trees,
The odor of the orange blooms,
The song of birds, and, more than these,
The silence of deserted rooms;

The respiration of the sea,
The soft caresses of the air,
All things in nature seemed to be
But ministers of her despair;

Till the o'erburdened heart, so long
Imprisoned in itself, found vent
And voice in one impassioned song
Of inconsolable lament.

Then as the sun, though hidden from sight,
Transmutes to gold the leaden mist,
Her life was interfused with light,
From realms that, though unseen, exist,

Inarime! Inarime!
Thy castle on the crags above
In dust shall crumble and decay,
But not the memory of her love.

THE REVENGE OF RAIN-IN-THE-FACE

In that desolate land and lone,
Where the Big Horn and Yellowstone
Roar down their mountain path,
By their fires the Sioux Chiefs
Muttered their woes and griefs
And the menace of their wrath.

"Revenge!" cried Rain-in-the-Face,
"Revenue upon all the race
Of the White Chief with yellow hair!"
And the mountains dark and high
From their crags re-echoed the cry
Of his anger and despair.

In the meadow, spreading wide
By woodland and riverside
The Indian village stood;
All was silent as a dream,
Save the rushing a of the stream
And the blue-jay in the wood.

In his war paint and his beads,
Like a bison among the reeds,
In ambush the Sitting Bull
Lay with three thousand braves
Crouched in the clefts and caves,
Savage, unmerciful!

Into the fatal snare
The White Chief with yellow hair
And his three hundred men
Dashed headlong, sword in hand;
But of that gallant band
Not one returned again.

The sudden darkness of death
Overwhelmed them like the breath
And smoke of a furnace fire:
By the river's bank, and between
The rocks of the ravine,
They lay in their bloody attire.

But the foemen fled in the night,
And Rain-in-the-Face, in his flight
Uplifted high in air

As a ghastly trophy, bore
The brave heart, that beat no more,
Of the White Chief with yellow hair.

Whose was the right and the wrong?
Sing it, O funeral song,
With a voice that is full of tears,
And say that our broken faith
Wrought all this ruin and scathe,
In the Year of a Hundred Years.

TO THE RIVER YVETTE

O lovely river of Yvette!
O darling river! like a bride,
Some dimpled, bashful, fair Lisette,
Thou goest to wed the Orge's tide.

Maincourt, and lordly Dampierre,
See and salute thee on thy way,
And, with a blessing and a prayer,
Ring the sweet bells of St. Forget.

The valley of Chevreuse in vain
Would hold thee in its fond embrace;
Thou glidest from its arms again
And hurriest on with swifter pace.

Thou wilt not stay; with restless feet
Pursuing still thine onward flight,
Thou goest as one in haste to meet
Her sole desire, her head's delight.

O lovely river of Yvette!
O darling stream! on balanced wings
The wood-birds sang the chansonnette
That here a wandering poet sings.

THE EMPEROR'S GLOVE

"Combien faudrait-il de peaux d'Espagne pour faire un gant de cette grandeur?" *A play upon the words gant, a glove, and Gand, the French for Ghent.*

On St. Baron's tower, commanding

Half of Flanders, his domain,
Charles the Emperor once was standing,
While beneath him on the landing
Stood Duke Alva and his train.

Like a print in books of fables,
Or a model made for show,
With its pointed roofs and gables,
Dormer windows, scrolls and labels,
Lay the city far below.

Through its squares and streets and alleys
Poured the populace of Ghent;
As a routed army rallies,
Or as rivers run through valleys,
Hurrying to their homes they went

"Nest of Lutheran misbelievers!"
Cried Duke Alva as he gazed;
"Haunt of traitors and deceivers,
Stronghold of insurgent weavers,
Let it to the ground be razed!"

On the Emperor's cap the feather
Nods, as laughing he replies:
"How many skins of Spanish leather,
Think you, would, if stitched together
Make a glove of such a size?"

A BALLAD OF THE FRENCH FLEET, OCTOBER, 1746

MR. THOMAS PRINCE loquitur

A fleet with flags arrayed
Sailed from the port of Brest,
And the Admiral's ship displayed
The signal: "Steer southwest."
For this Admiral D'Anville
Had sworn by cross and crown
To ravage with fire and steel
Our helpless Boston Town.

There were rumors in the street,
In the houses there was fear
Of the coming of the fleet,
And the danger hovering near.

And while from mouth to mouth
Spread the tidings of dismay,
I stood in the Old South,
Saying humbly: "Let us pray!

"O Lord! we would not advise;
But if in thy Providence
A tempest should arise
To drive the French fleet hence,
And scatter it far and wide,
Or sink it in the sea,
We should be satisfied,
And thine the glory be."

This was the prayer I made,
For my soul was all on flame,
And even as I prayed
The answering tempest came;
It came with a mighty power,
Shaking the windows and walls,
And tolling the bell in the tower,
As it tolls at funerals.

The lightning suddenly
Unsheathed its flaming sword,
And I cried: "Stand still, and see
The salvation of the Lord!"
The heavens were black with cloud,
The sea was white with hail,
And ever more fierce and loud
Blew the October gale.

The fleet it overtook,
And the broad sails in the van
Like the tents of Cushan shook,
Or the curtains of Midian.
Down on the reeling decks
Crashed the o'erwhelming seas;
Ah, never were there wrecks
So pitiful as these!

Like a potter's vessel broke
The great ships of the line;
They were carried away as a smoke,
Or sank like lead in the brine.
O Lord! before thy path
They vanished and ceased to be,
When thou didst walk in wrath

With thine horses through the sea!

Mounted on Kyrat strong and fleet,
His chestnut steed with four white feet,
Roushan Beg, called Kurroglou,
Son of the road and bandit chief,
Seeking refuge and relief,
Up the mountain pathway flew.

Such was Kyrat's wondrous speed,
Never yet could any steed
Reach the dust-cloud in his course.
More than maiden, more than wife,
More than gold and next to life
Roushan the Robber loved his horse.

In the land that lies beyond
Erzeroum and Trebizond,
Garden-girt his fortress stood;
Plundered khan, or caravan
Journeying north from Koordistan,
Gave him wealth and wine and food.

Seven hundred and fourscore
Men at arms his livery wore,
Did his bidding night and day.
Now, through regions all unknown,
He was wandering, lost, alone,
Seeking without guide his way.

Suddenly the pathway ends,
Sheer the precipice descends,
Loud the torrent roars unseen;
Thirty feet from side to side
Yawns the chasm; on air must ride
He who crosses this ravine.

Following close in his pursuit,
At the precipice's foot,
Reyhan the Arab of Orfah
Halted with his hundred men,
Shouting upward from the glen,
"La Illah illa Allah!"

Gently Roushan Beg caressed
Kyrat's forehead, neck, and breast;
Kissed him upon both his eyes;
Sang to him in his wild way,
As upon the topmost spray
Sings a bird before it flies.

"O my Kyrat, O my steed,
Round and slender as a reed,
Carry me this peril through!
Satin housings shall be thine,
Shoes of gold, O Kyrat mine,
O thou soul of Kurroglou!

"Soft thy skin as silken skein,
Soft as woman's hair thy mane,
Tender are thine eyes and true;
All thy hoofs like ivory shine,
Polished bright; O, life of mine,
Leap, and rescue Kurroglou!"

Kyrat, then, the strong and fleet,
Drew together his four white feet,
Paused a moment on the verge,
Measured with his eye the space,
And into the air's embrace
Leaped as leaps the ocean surge.

As the ocean surge o'er sand
Bears a swimmer safe to land,
Kyrat safe his rider bore;
Rattling down the deep abyss
Fragments of the precipice
Rolled like pebbles on a shore.

Roushan's tasselled cap of red
Trembled not upon his head,
Careless sat he and upright;
Neither hand nor bridle shook,
Nor his head he turned to look,
As he galloped out of sight.

Flash of harness in the air,
Seen a moment like the glare
Of a sword drawn from its sheath;
Thus the phantom horseman passed,
And the shadow that he cast
Leaped the cataract underneath.

Reyhan the Arab held his breath
While this vision of life and death
Passed above him. "Allahu!"
Cried he. "In all Koordistan
Lives there not so brave a man
As this Robber Kurroglou!"

HAROUN AL RASCHID

One day, Haroun Al Raschid read
A book wherein the poet said:--

"Where are the kings, and where the rest
Of those who once the world possessed?

"They're gone with all their pomp and show,
They're gone the way that thou shalt go.

"O thou who choosest for thy share
The world, and what the world calls fair,

"Take all that it can give or lend,
But know that death is at the end!"

Haroun Al Raschid bowed his head:
Tears fell upon the page he read.

KING TRISANKU

Viswamitra the Magician,
By his spells and incantations,
Up to Indra's realms elysian
Raised Trisanku, king of nations.

Indra and the gods offended
Hurled him downward, and descending
In the air he hung suspended,
With these equal powers contending.

Thus by aspirations lifted,
By misgivings downward driven,
Human hearts are tossed and drifted
Midway between earth and heaven.

A WRAITH IN THE MIST

"Sir, I should build me a fortification, if I
came to live here." --BOSWELL'S Johnson.

On the green little isle of Inchkenneth,
Who is it that walks by the shore,
So gay with his Highland blue bonnet,
So brave with his targe and claymore?

His form is the form of a giant,
But his face wears an aspect of pain;
Can this be the Laird of Inchkenneth?
Can this be Sir Allan McLean?

Ah, no! It is only the Rambler,
The Idler, who lives in Bolt Court,
And who says, were he Laird of Inchkenneth,
He would wall himself round with a fort.

THE THREE KINGS

Three Kings came riding from far away,
Melchior and Gaspar and Baltasar;
Three Wise Men out of the East were they,
And they travelled by night and they slept by day,
For their guide was a beautiful, wonderful star.

The star was so beautiful, large, and clear,
That all the other stars of the sky
Became a white mist in the atmosphere,
And by this they knew that the coming was near
Of the Prince foretold in the prophecy.

Three caskets they bore on their saddle-bows,
Three caskets of gold with golden keys;
Their robes were of crimson silk with rows
Of bells and pomegranates and furbelows,
Their turbans like blossoming almond-trees.

And so the Three Kings rode into the West,
Through the dusk of night, over hill and dell,
And sometimes they nodded with beard on breast

And sometimes talked, as they paused to rest,
With the people they met at some wayside well.

"Of the child that is born," said Baltasar,
"Good people, I pray you, tell us the news;
For we in the East have seen his star,
And have ridden fast, and have ridden far,
To find and worship the King of the Jews."

And the people answered, "You ask in vain;
We know of no king but Herod the Great!"
They thought the Wise Men were men insane,
As they spurred their horses across the plain,
Like riders in haste, and who cannot wait.

And when they came to Jerusalem,
Herod the Great, who had heard this thing,
Sent for the Wise Men and questioned them;
And said, "Go down unto Bethlehem,
And bring me tidings of this new king."

So they rode away; and the star stood still,
The only one in the gray of morn
Yes, it stopped, it stood still of its own free will,
Right over Bethlehem on the hill,
The city of David where Christ was born.

And the Three Kings rode through the gate and the guard,
Through the silent street, till their horses turned
And neighed as they entered the great inn-yard;
But the windows were closed, and the doors were barred,
And only a light in the stable burned.

And cradled there in the scented hay,
In the air made sweet by the breath of kine,
The little child in the manger lay,
The child, that would be king one day
Of a kingdom not human but divine.

His mother Mary of Nazareth
Sat watching beside his place of rest,
Watching the even flow of his breath,
For the joy of life and the terror of death
Were mingled together in her breast.

They laid their offerings at his feet:
The gold was their tribute to a King,
The frankincense, with its odor sweet,

Was for the Priest, the Paraclete,
The myrrh for the body's burying.

And the mother wondered and bowed her head,
And sat as still as a statue of stone;
Her heart was troubled yet comforted,
Remembering what the Angel had said
Of an endless reign and of David's throne.

Then the Kings rode out of the city gate,
With a clatter of hoofs in proud array;
But they went not back to Herod the Great,
For they knew his malice and feared his hate,
And returned to their homes by another way.

SONG

Stay, stay at home, my heart, and rest;
Home-keeping hearts are happiest,
For those that wander they know not where
Are full of trouble and full of care;
To stay at home is best.

Weary and homesick and distressed,
They wander east, they wander west,
And are baffled and beaten and blown about
By the winds of the wilderness of doubt;
To stay at home is best.

Then stay at home, my heart, and rest;
The bird is safest in its nest;
O'er all that flutter their wings and fly
A hawk is hovering in the sky;
To stay at home is best.

THE WHITE CZAR

The White Czar is Peter the Great. Batyushka, Father dear, and Gosudar, Sovereign, are titles the Russian people are fond of giving to the Czar in their popular songs.

Dost thou see on the rampart's height
That wreath of mist, in the light
Of the midnight moon? O, hist!
It is not a wreath of mist;

It is the Czar, the White Czar,
Batyushka! Gosudar!

He has heard, among the dead,
The artillery roll o'erhead;
The drums and the tramp of feet
Of his soldiery in the street;
He is awake! the White Czar,
Batyushka! Gosudar!

He has heard in the grave the cries
Of his people: "Awake! arise!"
He has rent the gold brocade
Whereof his shroud was made;
He is risen! the White Czar,
Batyushka! Gosudar!

From the Volga and the Don
He has led his armies on,
Over river and morass,
Over desert and mountain pass;
The Czar, the Orthodox Czar,
Batyushka! Gosudar!

He looks from the mountain-chain
Toward the seas, that cleave in twain
The continents; his hand
Points southward o'er the land
Of Roumili! O Czar,
Batyushka! Gosudar!

And the words break from his lips:
"I am the builder of ships,
And my ships shall sail these seas
To the Pillars of Hercules!
I say it; the White Czar,
Batyushka! Gosudar!

"The Bosphorus shall be free;
It shall make room for me;
And the gates of its water-streets
Be unbarred before my fleets.
I say it; the White Czar,
Batyushka! Gosudar!

"And the Christian shall no more
Be crushed, as heretofore,
Beneath thine iron rule,

O Sultan of Istamboul!
I swear it; I the Czar,
Batyushka! Gosudar!"

DELIA

Sweet as the tender fragrance that survives,
When martyred flowers breathe out their little lives,
Sweet as a song that once consoled our pain,
But never will be sung to us again,
Is thy remembrance. Now the hour of rest
Hath come to thee. Sleep, darling; it is best.

www.ingramcontent.com/pod-product-compliance
Lightning Source LLC
Chambersburg PA
CBHW060143050426
42448CB00010B/2280